MARINE

MARINE

Alan Jenkins and John Kinsella

ENITHARMON PRESS

First published in 2015
by Enitharmon Press
10 Bury Place
London WC1A 2JL

www.enitharmon.co.uk

Distributed in the UK by
Central Books
99 Wallis Road
London E9 5LN

Distributed in the USA and Canada
by Independent Publishers Group
814 North Franklin Street
Chicago, IL 60610
USA
www.ipgbook.com

ISBN: 978-1-910392-07-2

ISBN: 978-1-910392-21-8 (signed limited edition of 35 hardback copies, clothbound at The Fine Book Bindery)

Enitharmon Press gratefully acknowledges the financial support of Arts Council England, through Grants for the Arts.

Individuals contribute to sustain the Press through the Enitharmon Friends Scheme. We are deeply grateful to all Friends, particularly our Patrons: Colin Beer, Sean O'Connor and those who wished to remain anonymous.

British Library Cataloguing-in-Publication Data.
A catalogue record for this book is available
from the British Library.

Designed in Albertina by Libanus Press
and printed in England by
Short Run Press

CONTENTS

Razorshell Wreck on Barleycove Beach on the Eve of All Saints' Day 9

The little cruiser chugged past Faversham 10

On Alfred Wallis's *Barque With a Man at the Wheel On a Stormy Sea* (1936–38) 13

Now the grey-green briny slopped through my hull 14

Two Black Boats Sailing Up Dark Grey Waves 15

The jagged lee-shore loomed 16

On Alfred Wallis's *Black Steamship* (1934–38) 17

The Ravished Heart 18

Figurehead 19

Mermaid 20

On the Figurehead of *The Old Victry* (a painting by Alfred Wallis) 21

Sailors 22

Painted Bellows 26

Marsh-Woman 27

Looking Out to Sea, Prevelly Park, 1974 28

Sea-Voices 29

Natural Bridge, Torndirrup, 1967 30

The Drunken Boat 32

Le Piton des Neiges 36

Bats at Grand Fond 40

Cabots sauteurs 41

Catamaran Works to Round Pointe des Aigrettes 42

Tropicbirds 43

The sea is wild today and the no swim signs are up everywhere 44
La Mer cassée 45
I knew this path through cypresses, an olive-grove 46
The Bourbon Baudelaire 47
In my new life I am the skipper 51
Passage Through Icebergs (painted as *Voyage to Labrador* by Alfred Wallis, 1935–6) 52
Log 54
Carraiglea Aubade 56
Long After (*Jean Genet*) 57
Carraiglea 58
Spree 59
Out of the Cottage's Big Feature Windows 60
Ship of Fools 61
Charter 63
Yaravi 64
Wrecked Spanish Galleon and Vestigial Property and Identity Anxieties 66
Lost 69
Figurehead of the Clipper *Samuel Plimsoll* 71
Long After (*Euaristos Kalfas*) 73
Emptied Vessel 74
Anointed, sweat-streaked, reddened, raw 75
Full Moon Over Long Island Bay 76
I was in irons. The bulkheads groaned; and then a lull 77
Albatross 79
Selkies Lashing the Rocks 80

Wild 81
I knew this path, the promenade, the lanes 82
The Pragmatism of Inland Birds 83
Mute Swans Over Carraiglea 84
Sharks 85
Lot's Wife 89
Mermaid *(The Sailor's Memory)* 90
Port 93
I knew this path, a thin brown arm around the cliff 94
St Ives 95
Long After *(Julien Gracq)* 97
Brise marine 98
Sea-Music 99
Belle Étoile 102

RAZORSHELL WRECK ON BARLEYCOVE BEACH ON THE EVE OF ALL SAINTS' DAY

A small wreck is a large wreck when a species is in retreat,
undertow and wave-sets soothe and stress between slate hills:
the rise & fall, the artwork re-inscribed in sand which will
gradually wash away, the full weight of the Atlantic.

So attuned, so sensitive, so determined to pull themselves down –
foot anchored hydraulic pull to start again down down down –
razorshell feedertube sucking low-tide sweet and sour
into the glasses-case body, enrapture, huddling organs

snug against a cut-throat world's predators, the larger shifts
making small changes massive, prescribe low-tide second-sight,
test hope as St Jude's Day swell ripped the world apart, a mass
of brethren exposed to make detritus of selves, the soup

of origins and excrescence sharply in bands of shifting light,
dozens scattered on this earthquake beach, this *harbour wave* jewel
where corpses cut bare feet to bone or sinew, ghouls and gods
make sense of spring-water bottles and plastic ropes binding

'best kept secrets'. So many starved here, and razorshells make
discrete sub-fences that will briefly hold the residue of Lisbon's collapse,
a history divined in shell, its dead reflections, separations along
vaguely perfect faultlines, what fate saw from below the sand.

THE LITTLE CRUISER CHUGGED PAST FAVERSHAM

The little cruiser chugged past Faversham, upstream on the Swale;
Diesel, bilge and backwash and a stink of adolescent male
Filled the wheelhouse as I ran her shattered bows into the shale.

'*Hurrumph.*' The tannoy screeched and rasped and spluttered into life
And from it came a voice I knew: '*You boy! Get it cut! Or – or –*'
(His hand had gripped a hank of hair): '*Or give me that sail-knife!*'

That long-dead master-mariner! So hugely-eared
He could have gull-winged down the rope-hung corridor,
Who growled his orders through a nicotine-flecked beard,

Who barked at us through yellow teeth clenched on his pipe
Now scowled at me and grunted, 'And how is our little whore
Of Babylon? I've got your measure, boy, I know your type.

Remember summer evenings with that stink at ebb and flood –
Not of post-match changing rooms, stale jock-straps, staler socks
But rotting gulls and fish-heads on the bottle-littered mud

Where treasure-twitchers picked through tidal leavings, pungent silt? –
The sewer-sump that was the Thames, the bilge of Surrey Docks?
The greenish wood at waterline, froth that factories had spilt?

I've seen you hoist a tattered sail, jib and tack and navigate
Among the shoals and sheltered moles owned by the drinking classes,
In the stews of Notting Dale, in Portobello's narrow strait;
I've seen you search midshipmen's souls while eyeing up their pretty arses.

I've seen you come about and heave to in the chill of early morning
As you used to do, a motley crew, at Wapping Stair when day was dawning
After shipping grog all night in Muldoon's with the bo'sun,
Mick, and Kydd, first mate; after trying tricks you learnt in Chosun

Down below with Moll or Kate. Remember all the knocks and shocks
You took in bare-knuckle fights behind the boating sheds?
Remember when those big pressed men, your shipmates, grabbed their cocks
And tossed themselves off, leering, to your cheering in the heads?

The harbour at Rangoon! Indecision on the poop!
The sea roads not taken! And that ship of fools, your little sloop…
True north, Trafalgar, trade routes, polar circumnavigation –
Things that might have made a man of you! Your birthright and your nation!

Today at fifty-five you feel your daemon has been trapped;
The time-wasting, skirt-chasing years when nothing scanned;
Everything you are and care for standing ready to be scrapped

Like *Ark Royal* and half the fleet. The sea-roads not taken!
The shadows on the wave-ridged, gull-flecked, glistening sand;
The captains and the shipmates gone, the quiet berths forsaken!

Now I see your flag flying at half-mast, and wonder why?
The burden of their memory, who "must not altogether die"?
Or of the knowledge, late-acquired, that you yourself must die?

Or is it that you think of England, of her historic wrecks
And of her people fed on lies and lotteries and sex,
The shit-showers of stupidity that rain down on her decks?

Now England loves, when brought low by defeat or death or fright
Not quiet consolation in the watches of the night
But to make an exhibition of herself when she's tight;

She loves the march-past (rather than the past), the flags
And flowers on coffins, the weeping and the body-bags,
The raw emotion and the chat-show cheer, the awful gags

Of slappers, slags; the rolling English drunkard and the vulgar
English tongue. Who now expects that, as once at Trafalgar,
Every man shall do…? Who now can recall its fulgor?'

Then he faded, with the shore where he'd tarnished at quiet anchor,
With the wharves and sheds, the rigs and derricks and the tanker
He had captained, and my 'shipmates' shouting *Wanker!*…

ON ALFRED WALLIS'S *BARQUE WITH A MAN AT THE WHEEL ON A STORMY SEA* (1936–38)

This is what I dream, inland,
Perched on the hillside, leeward,
Bush volatile and the heat peeling
Away layers. A grey-blue world,
Ocean and a sky that is an ocean
As well. A three-masted barque
And a man on the verge of fifty
At the wheel: not struggling,
And too sure of himself, taking
For granted a lifetime of skill,
His crew all below deck, un-
Wanted. I have been compiling
Stories of the oceans. Waves
Are heavy and break the gunwales,
The sails well-sewn but ghostly.
This quasi-nightmare I cannot
Wake from I will steer through.
And, in truth, it's not *grey-blue*
Nor *steely*, and has no colour:
Salt and krill in the eyes,
Night and storm blindness.
I'll – we'll – get through,
But what landfall awaits me,
And who will be there to greet us?

NOW THE GREY-GREEN BRINY SLOPPED THROUGH MY HULL

Now the grey-green briny slopped through my hull
And sluiced my planking, stained with the blood
And rotgut I'd puked up; strafed by a single gull,
Like a hulk when high water creeps up the mud

To lap around it where it lies, I awoke
But the steering gear had gone, the starboard stays
Were rusted through, dark rot patched the varnished oak
Of my timbers, the log was missing several torn-off days…

The louring sky, the sudden squalls dismayed me,
The jagged lee-shore off my starboard beam.
And that long-familiar, long-lost voice belayed me:
'Are you the same suburban boy whose dream

Was not to set sail in *Gypsy Moth III*
From Greenwich to Durban via Finisterre
With Sir Francis Chichester, to master the sea,
But to take wine with Byron, opium with Baudelaire?

Look at you now! Your verse bobs like a yacht
In heavy seas, it veers and bobs and weaves
As if the helmsman were unfit, a soak, a sot;
In its wake the wash an empty vessel leaves…

"England expects" is the signal that one sends
But what *you* expect is somehow to stay afloat
And somehow not to have to make amends
For what can't be undone, for the little boat

You sailed on the municipal pond, and sank,
For the endless rounds that killed your friends,
For those who were abandoned on the bank –
For all who loved you, and met watery ends!'…

TWO BLACK BOATS SAILING UP DARK GREY WAVES (AFTER ALFRED WALLIS)

Dark grey waves take you nowhere
fast and deep you're going, have gone
where you come from, a driving force
a weighty concern, never conducive
to arrival or departure for all their pace
and compulsion, record of signature lost,
signing-off your warrant your papers
as fingerprints rub off, rope burnt,
surging, tilting and hauling: expectation,
certainty; the stomach a crystal ball
of swell to slosh so persistently,
predictably at a pitch around the ball
of our planet: a coastal cliff or beckoning
mass of rock just surfaces to dash against,
keeping bow and sprit aligned to enter
to leave to confront be pursued but show
no better side to overhang, the ledge:
what's not dust is liquid is mud:
in all seas experience sails instinct,
learning, superstition, the tying-off
of knots and trimming of sails
(I've had my encounters) stretched
between boats too close in fate in fact,
black with shades and those shadows,
shadows of those bruising waves.

THE JAGGED LEE-SHORE LOOMED

The jagged lee-shore loomed. Had I picked up a dose
Of trouble from that pick-up in the last port of call –
And was that Porto, Portobello or Porthcawl?
What did it matter? The two of us had not been close…

I'd hoped for so long to be, once more, under sail
And tacking into harbour, rich with smells of rope and tar
But I was not alone, the air I sniffed was stale
No-air, sweat-and-tobacco, drinkers' breath – a bar!

One in which I'd often had to navigate
The reef, the rock that should be off the stern
(The stews of Wapping, Portobello's narrow strait!)
And learned to expect the unexpected turn

Of events, of the tide…. 'Those nights are gone;
You've been in the wind and rain of your inner weather
For so long, you've barely noticed what's been going on.
I'd say it was time you got your act together.

You never understood that it ain't no good…'
This was a woman's voice, with words that flayed me:
'Whenever you go out, in your little craft of wood,
Your little craft of words, it will be me you hear

Reminding you of how you scorned your mother
And all the others who loved you – God knows why –
It will be me reminding you that you will die,
It will be me reminding you of everything you fear….'

ON ALFRED WALLIS'S *BLACK STEAMSHIP* (1934–38)

What blackness holds the white steam
In its black funnel; heavy, dense
Smoke out of the funnel, the sea taking
On the ironclad character, bearing its weight,
Its progress? I am reminded of the metal
Fire-fighter's tank my grandfather
Of the forests left to my father in his will.
Metal tank strapped to the back, webbed
To cotton and flesh, black rubber hose,
Brass nozzle, pressured by pumping
To spray a mist, or squirt a jet. Maybe
A language of boiler rooms and steam
Ships? To fight forest-fires, dozens
Of men formed a phalanx, each watching
The exposed side of their neighbour,
Watery shields melded. Futile as walls
Of flame bore down. Inside the furnace,
The charring, the black residue. Fire
On everyone's lips as the southern half
Of a country smoulders, burns. Newspapers
And amateurs record images. The steam-
Ship ploughs through contrary but willing
Waters. The terracotta of ancient fires
Spread around: a definitive presence.

THE RAVISHED HEART

(after Rimbaud)

My sad heart slobbers on the poop,
My heart all black-tobacco-blue;
They chuck at it their gobs of gloop,
My sad heart slobbering on the poop –
Under the piss-taking of this crew
Who laugh themselves to death it's true
My sad heart slobbers on the poop,
My heart all black-tobacco-blue.

Ithyphallic, squaddie-like
Their pissy little jokes have fucked it.
In the wheelhouse, carved with a spike
They left the legend, squaddie-like:
Jenkins loves my cock, and sucked it.
Abracadabra! Waves, conduct it
To be washed (my heart, I mean); it's like,
Their pissy little jokes have fucked it.

When they have chewed their baccy dry
What shall we do, my heart, old shag?
There'll be Bacchic hiccups by and by
When they have chewed their baccy dry;
I'll heave up my guts, sky-high,
Me, if it doesn't make them gag.
When they have chewed their baccy dry,
What shall we do, my heart, old shag?

FIGUREHEAD

I thought I saw one being buffeted and tossed
In dark surf on a beach near Geraldton. Fifteen,
And skindiving with a mate under a full moon,
Where silt in the water was the only illumination
In seas choppy over reef; bands of ribbonweed
Crossing ankles above flippers filling my head
With seasnakes, I propelled myself back to shore,
Knocked about by mid-sized breakers carving
The beach, snorkel, mask and buoyant skin,
Leaden middle a fulcrum for surf. A lady lifted
Like Marianne out of the foam, but washed
Of tricolours and with a split that drew her
Eyes apart, her breasts ghostly and smooth
Against the wormy wood of her torso, splintering
Sand and phosphorescence. I reached out for her,
Trident in hand – an offering or parody – but
She flinched back into the sea and I stumbled,
James Bond pantomime, Fool of the Deep,
Mask sloshing behind the glass that fogs,
That you clear with spit, and Marianne's breasts
Out of reach, so treacherous free of their bondage
Below bowsprit, de-masted wreck flailing
On aquarium floor, bust carved out of air
And soil and forests of France, ship gone down
Unrecorded, haunting as violence and sex.

MERMAID

Aged four, I was hypnotized by swirls
Of white foam in the waves, their film of slime;
By fronds of weed that swayed in rock-pools, girls'
Drifting hair... *What's he doing all this time?* –
The words my mother called out, ten years on,
As I sat tugging at my raw, stiff, straining cock
(The bathwater going cold, the light already gone),
Remembering that strange girl leaning on a rock,
Pulling up her jeans – the sudden, startling blur
Against the pale skin of her narrow thighs,
A pointed dark isosceles of fur;
Still in store, the unrepeatable surprise,
All that lay out of sight, beyond, inside:
Slithery bivalve, quick-darting fishes, salt tide.

ON THE FIGUREHEAD OF *THE OLD VICTRY* (A PAINTING BY ALFRED WALLIS)

From memory, what will be will *bee,*
Effigy reaching out to the pale swell
Nursing the *great* three-master warship
Tethered below an empty sky. Description
Fills imagination of where figurehead
Reaches, portending layers of gundecks,
Bowsprit that would lift into heavens: nexus
Between eras of defence and conquest.
No seraphim and cherubim, but one
Fellow reaching down through surface.
But even a gently surging harbour sea
Close to shore holds the vast weight
Of world on shoulders, sea legs on land,
House swaying like a hammock.
Company? Flags stiff with the breeze.
And there's nothing *naive* about fate:
When the sails are packed away
The rigging plays the weight of vastness.
Figurehead reaching out with stick arms,
Its posture male, as if the loss of women
Is too hard to trawl from the deep,
Murmuring out of the escutcheon:
Honi Soit Qui Mal Y Pense.

SAILORS

(after Tristan Corbière)

Gilbert & Sullivan sailors caught in the glare
Of footlights, in their sky-blue frock-coats, swear
By a thousand portholes! While outside on
The street, the terminal veteran of *HMS Gone*
But Not Forgotten flogs the stuff that kills
Dead rats. *Youngster crippled in one arm –*
At sea, no less – *fallen on hard times, who fills*
His empty days with singing, since his shipwreck;
The woman in the salt-water pool who tries to calm
The waves by waving at them; Captain Bird'seye on the quarter-deck;
These aren't sailors! – Sailors – what sudden, twitchy spurt
Engendered them, who even in a race not far from dirt
Are a race apart? The way they put all *landlubbers*
In the same boat! A *floozie and some rubbers*
Are waiting in my hammock; while what you get
In your bed's a parson's prayers, tears and sweat . . .

What do we know of them, these reef-knotted types?
Dry land makes them sea-sick; they're as useless there
As web-footed birds deprived of water, air.
As foul in the breeches as their stinking pipes.
They feel they're rolling with the rollers that they miss:
Ashore, you can't get sober on the piss!

We don't know them. What's it mean to them, 'ashore'?
A bit of R & R, and booze, and brawls,
The hospital, the prison, and a whore.
As for the rest. . . A *long way from sea-squalls,*
Aren't we? Them, they're *sailors*. Wracks and storms,
Hazards, accidents, adventures of all forms
Have left their hatchet faces with a nervous tic
Of reflex scorn for all that isn't *them*...

They're A-OK! They're men, from stern to stem!
They have the ocean; you, your landlubber *schtick*,
Flowerbeds and lintels; *footslogger*, in a word –
Pipe-clay and mouldy feet – that's right. You heard.

Them, they're *old salts* and *the sea-coast's brothers*,
Heart-on-sleeve and hand-on-heart, swear on their mothers,
Sturdy constitutions, up for it – up for it all!
Can you say as much? They aren't what you'd call
Quite the thing. Maybe they have sweethearts round here,
Stuff going on the rozzer turns a blind eye to
As he stops them at the door and waves them through –
Come on, you need a cast-iron stomach and no fear
To go in there in broad daylight – in 'Cape Horn',
As they call that cat-house in their sun-baked lingo;
Cape Horn, black hole of hailstorms – and to chew
On the bit of meat they grab, to which they cling-O,
Without wanting to throw up; to chew that flesh
Like a tobacco-plug, or some deal from Marrakesh!
Half-finished angels, children, hard, forlorn,
Throwing to the winds the tenderness they brim with
And the lousy pay they buy their bit of quim with,
They troop in as if to mass, or to the Ark –
Their faces part-infant-Jesus and part-shark.

They love extravagantly – love the hunchback's hump,
The open wound, the Virgin and the Plod they thump;
They pray to everything; but their favourite prayer
's to the coat that duffed-up blue-coat-Saviours wear...
Come on – the tough guy who gets in your face
Also knows who's boss; retains an inborn grace –

Hewn from one block of wood! The good little boy
And the bad dog, his master's pride and joy!

Back home on board, these brutes have their poetry –
Their songs dredged from a soul lashed to the sea,
Soused, ecstatic songs, made up on the fo'c'sle watch…
Heedless, each a living poem (or a botch…)

And always, for their mums, the *lovely old dear,*
These heroes of deprivation shed a childish tear;
Tears of love for their *sweetness and light.* For in
Their own country – however far away –
They have, these types with beaten-copper skin,
Someone who waits: the pale fiancée
They abandoned one day for the ocean wave.
She waits in uncertainty – they're so far apart.
He has her name tattooed with a skewered heart
On his arm... O the sea is deep and wide,
The sea's a jealous lover who can moan and rave;
Maybe she'll be widowed before she's a bride.
But she'll still be proud that she can say,
Through her sobs, *He was a sailor!* to her dying day…

Faced with a big sea, he's more than man enough,
This sailor-all-the-way-through! – Look at him:
One foot on the crumbling bridge, sober, tough,
That's how he'll end up: simple, noble, tackle trim,
A hole in the water! No frills or flowers…

Some – survivors of scurvy or shit-showers,
Flotsam from old wrecks – come back, disfigured,
Crippled, mashed, out of it; minus one eye
(*To your one extra?*), plus yellow fever (*Yours*
Is the pink sort?), scar (*Well I'll be jiggered*),
Fucked-up arm (*A surgeon was the cause*),

Hole in one cheek (*Marlin spike, but I won't die*).
Come on, they don't make hulls like this one any more!
I've swung from the yard-arm twice...On which note
The good-citizen-freebooter takes out his knife
To chip away at a little child's toy boat.

So they live on, if you can call it life,
Sniffing the air for signs of lousy weather,
Rich on a pension of a few hundred quid,
Old cartridge-cases, salvage from what heroes did –
The glory of it all! – *Heroes? Guffaw!*
No, thanks: we're sailors. Matelots, for ever!

Dream on, sailors; dream, as you pace the deck
In the long night-watches, the peaceful dreams of men
Who hear the ribbing groan and the cracked mast
Let out a scream – no, that's long passed,
It's gone for good. *Farewell, the fine three-master*
Festooned with flags, and every other wreck!

Like an old hulk, stripped of rigging, high and dry
That still feels wavelets lapping round it when
The tide creeps up across the stinking mud,
So the stranded sea-soul waits in torment. – Waits to die?
– *No, for the flood.*

PAINTED BELLOWS (AFTER ALFRED WALLIS)

The dead lung breathes
without a will of its own;
a trick of forgotten thought,
a knee-jerk reaction. By the dark
fireplace – before first light chills
panes and water, the necromancy
of seas and tide, harbour and boat –
the pursed lips blow hard
into embers: a false sun
throws light just as the tide
bluffs recovery. In our mind's eye,
our breath frozen on the window,
we blow up a storm.

MARSH-WOMAN

Now that I go with any Beatrice or plain Beth,
Now I have forgotten her, the little clam
Of her cunt, the wine that clung to her breath,

Now I have forgotten who I am
And who she was, and how things were,
This wind off the estuary, the salt-marsh she knew

Like the back of her hand, it cannot hurt
Any more than those fading memories do –
Of the back of her hand as she tugged my shirt,

Of her dance to the cheering of the crew,
Of her forward-falling tits and hair
Above me on my bunk, the sounds she made,

Her sudden floods – and what do I care
If such things now mean even less to her
Than they do to me? That as they fade

From memory they lose their edges, blur
Like the estuary dropping out of view
Or the salt-marsh in mist? And that is death.

LOOKING OUT TO SEA, PREVELLY PARK, 1974

Look out or back, unfinding anger or pleasure,
big expanse to wonder and 'maze, counteract
a singular measure: body shape to hold such
aspiration, to blow conch or snuggle
in nacre; a wrecking lust, a wandering
blast, all wishes to grow into: side by side
with younger and older, so much older,
to bind that chromosomal ocean.

Generations of waves tune reef,
smaller sets make do with swell
to beach. Lesser bladders of weed
decorate points of advent and exodus,
but all is contingent, and so those signature-
ploys of feet. Fresh layers of cloud
apply as old layers dry. Sky-sea-air
parody, and dangerous nets of thought.

From transparent points of contact,
residue after white horse's froth,
green silhouettes of sand and sandfish,
turquoise to ominous navy blue
of coral and wrecks, the weight
of conflict submerged. And no seabirds
anywhere to pierce the breeze, support
its weight on sea-heavy wings.

SEA-VOICES

When I knelt to prise up a smooth, striped pebble
And saw weed-coloured crabs scuttle sideways,
Carrying their backs – it was terrible,
How quickly they were gone before my eyes
In a swirl of water, a puff of sand –
Cut-throat razor-clams, barnacles like coolies' hats
And the sea-anemone that closed tight
When I touched it, all lay in wait for my plunging hand;
A wind blew that voice across the mudflats,
How much of life you'll spend on the sea-floor,
How frail they are, your little craft of wood,
Your little craft of words…
                                        Now the shore
Is washed away – a spume of white
As, lashed by unseen nets, tonight
I walk beside it, hunched figure in a hood
That hides my face like the one I wore
The night she waved goodbye for good.
You could lose yourself there, drown
Where neither shout nor whispered word unlocks
Help from cannonades of air. Go down,
Everything is awash, go down to the rocks.

NATURAL BRIDGE, TORNDIRRUP, 1967

Broken cog of coastline, teeth chipped, wheel
petrified into mechanism of continent.
The stone is hard enough to defer time.
Barefoot, he stands where no one will
stand now: angles have shifted and 'at
an angle' is a new trigonometry.

It's a fiercely windy place, then as now.
Not a hair out of place, the neat sweep
away from a parting. He remembers
that of his father, his father's faith in Brylcreem.
The reason for being there, the Main Feature –
bridge of rock where king waves
might leap through its mouth – isn't
featured, or at least not with its best face
showing. Case of sublime suppression.

Small child a focus of attention.
A section of the bridge has since
collapsed into the cavernous ocean
but it's not there anyway, solid as creation.
And the steep headland (in black and white),
looks more jagged with channels to wave-line
setting up its years of smoothing-out, erosion
that will style the coast for tourism.

Vanguard portraiture landscape.
A weight of visitors. Granite quarried
and smoothed and stacked by stormy revolutions.
His right foot has a slight turn we'll hope
to correct. The sand and stone beneath his feet
etch his feet. A pyrography. A mapping.
Child placed to take in his surroundings
to replay for his own children. A plan.

As now he watches hundreds of flashes
blind the Rosetta Stone; not studying texture,
reaching through glass case to touch in thought.
Capturing data to be filed for later use, to dredge
up when a new language calls out for the old,
to calibrate the stone we build out of, those
vast and formative oceans we cross.

THE DRUNKEN BOAT

(after Rimbaud)

As I nosed down the placid river I could feel
The towropes slacken – screaming redskins had made off
With the boatmen and nailed them naked, hand and heel,
To painted stakes for target practice. The trade-off:

How I no longer gave a toss for them, that gang
Who'd loaded me with Flemish wheat or English twill.
When they were done with, like the song the redskins sang,
The river let me make my own way down, at will.

All winter, I was as deaf to reason as a child –
The anchor, helm and log had long gone overboard.
Lording it over choppy waters, going wild,
I ran with them! – surges, peninsulas unmoored;

Bobbed like a cork on waves that engulfed a tanker –
The hurricanes that blessed my awakenings at sea! –
And, as I danced on those rolling billows, sank her;
Not once did I long for harbour-lights to welcome me.

The greenish water slopping through my hull's soft pine,
Sweeter than windfalls are to kids, sluiced all the blood
I'd puked up off my planking, and the dirt-cheap wine;
Left me as rudderless as driftwood on the flood.

Since then, I have bathed in the poem of the sea,
A milkiness infused with stars, and blue-green deeps
Through which a drowned man sometimes drifts down, dreamily,
Pallid, spellbound flotsam; where, in blue mulatto sleeps,

The slumped or fevered sleeps, the bright slow burn of day,
Headier than absinthe, more viral than our verse,

A sudden stain on all that brilliant blue-grey,
The rust-blood-reds of love ferment their bitter curse.

I've seen the low sun, soiled with freakish horrors, cast
Its light on welts, coagulations, purple-blue;
Waves like actors in some drama of the ancient past
Unrolling slatted blinds a shudder ripples through!

I've dreamed the emerald night with drifts of dazzled snow,
Slow rise of kisses to the sea's eyes, unheard-of
Saps circulating in the bloodstream, blue-yellow
Dawn-light, phosphorescence-choirs! Surf like a herd of

Frightened cattle, bellowing and snorting round the rocks:
I've gone on chasing after it for months on end
But never dreamt Our Ladies in luminous frocks
Could muzzle the waters they walked on, take the wind

Out of that stampede…Rainbows stretched taut like bridles
Round great grey-green herds below the seas' horizon,
Unimagined Cubas, where a flower idles
In the skin of men, a flower with panthers' eyes on!

I've seen collapsing sea-floors, roaring hollows born
Of flat calms, lightning-bolts that cracked apart the skies;
Tide-rips, cataracts, whirlpools, waterspouts, the dawn
That lifted like a flock of doves. With my own eyes

I've seen what men sometimes suppose they really saw! –
Enormous swamps fermenting, and a great sperm whale
Rotting in the reeds; undulations of the shore,
Some deep gulf where ships, run aground on banks of shale,

Break up while giant tick-infested snakes uncurl
From tortured trees, in wafts of black stench; skies as hot
As glowing braziers; waves of mother-of-pearl,
Silver-plated suns, glaciers of azure snot.

I should have liked to show the children those great fish
Of the blue wave, the golden fish, the fish that sing.
Foam-flowers have cradled my sea-drifts, and the swish
Of unseen winds has more than once helped me take wing.

Sometimes, a martyr to the poles and latitudes
The sea's sobs rocked me gently, and it showed me these:
Shadow-blooms, with yellow suckers – such lassitudes! . . .
I kept still as a praying woman on her knees.

An island, almost, but one whose rowdy beaches
Had been colonized by yellow-eyed squabbling birds.
I was gull-winging through a storm of shit and screeches
When they passed the frayed ropes – the drowned, sinking backwards

In their sleep! Now I, wreck caught in the tangled hair
Of creeks and inlets, flung up by the hurricane
Into the ether, into blue and birdless air,
Whose water-sodden carcass neither coastguard's plane

Nor rich man's yacht would have picked up on their radar;
Free and risen, reeking, from the purple spume, I
Who pierced the reddened wall that streams with blue catarrh
And – proper poets' treats – sun-lichen-growths, the sky;

Who scudded, black sea-horses for escort, half-crazed
Flotsam flecked by little undersea lights, across
The ultramarine of skies that summer, as it blazed,
Rammed into throats as hot as smokestacks; who would toss

And turn and tremble when I heard, fifty leagues away,
Slow churn of maelstroms, moan of rutting Behemoths;
Threading the glassy blue for ever and a day,
I hanker for old Europe, the ramparts of the Goths!

I've seen star-archipelagos, ecstatic isles'
High heavens open to the rider of the waves.
The unplumbed nights: is that where you sleep your exile's
Sleep, O million gilded birds, Life in autoclaves?

True, fuck it: I've wept buckets. Daybreaks break my heart.
Every moon is torment; bitter every sun.
Sour love has drugged, bloated me. O that my strakes could part,
My keel split, and I go down! . . . If I long for *one*

Of Europe's waters, it's this one: on his haunches
Beside that cold black puddle, a sad little boy,
As the scented twilight comes on, squats and launches
A boat as frail as a butterfly – his paper toy.

Steeped in the languorous swell, I can't, any more,
Tack in the big barges' wake, or lift the clipper's prize
Or breast the proud flags and the flapping pennants; nor
Drift past the prison hulks, beneath their hollow eyes.

LE PITON DES NEIGES

To my friend A. Lionnet
(after Auguste Lacaussade)

Ocean, Ocean, when your fuming waves
Lift, roaring, making one majestic wave
From foaming heads, rearing up to air,
Appearing to touch the sky with its sublime crest;
We see its peak smoking like a vast
Crater, its huge mass mastering the waters!

The furrows that its volume compresses,
Come in fury to smash themselves at its base;
The wave rises and leaps towards its arrogant
Brow; but this one – see! – like the God of the tempest,
With foam and vapours crowns its crest,
And seems to dominate its furious aspect.

Just as in these places you prevail,
Glorious Salazian mountain, just
As from nearby mountains your aerial
Forehead towers, juts, projects!
Immense, motionless, eternal
From the high centre of my isle,
Your summit, calm and noble,
Imposes and commands the gaze;
Seat of an eternal winter,
The wind besieging your
Face covered in snow and hoar-
Frost like old men's heads.

From the cradle of the deep seas,
The eye that perceives your virile beauty,
There, upon the green daughter of the waves,
Loves your splendid decay.
And you seem in your silence

To listen to the noise in the skies
Of the gentle, swaying breeze
Or of the rushing north wind;
Or like a lone colossus,
Fixing a centenarian's gaze
Upon the earth and the waves,
To dream, grave and soundless!

When day dies and shadows appear,
When the moon rises above cloud,
The ocean at your feet shines like a mirror;
From the skies, night's orb whitens vast domes
And you see ships like white phantoms,
Sliding along the horizon under evening's vapours
And the poor fisherman whose swift boat
Bounds lightly upon the liquid pasture
And the seabird surprised by night,
Perceive your peak from a great distance,
Navigating by your sublime summit,
Advancing cradled by the air's breath.

And from afar on the immense sea,
By the dreaming moon's rays,
The voyager's startled eye
Contemplates you in silence.
The straying cloud that halts,
Seems to stir upon your summit,
As one sees floating upon their
Heads white plumes of heroes;
And your ancient and profound mass
Flooded by a gentle brightness
Seems to be the blue spectre

Of wave upright on the waves' abyss!
Ah! how many centuries have passed
Before your wrinkled face?
Yet time's footfall is erased
From your ravaged peak.
How many days of calm and cyclone,
And of cloud and sun,
And of shipwreck and pain,
Have glimmered before your ancient eye?
Tempest, shadow, north wind, light,
All returned to primeval night,
But you with your immense height,
You were then as you are today!

Then, as now, morning's first light,
And vanishing day's last light,
Spread out their fires on your azure countenance;
And when dawn or night come to smile over
The world, you alone shone in the ethereal empire,
Like a lighthouse with soft and soundless glints.
Then, as now, from your sterile rocks
You poured pure and limpid torrents onto our fields;
And, ever defying the destroying tempest,
Draping your bare flanks with a cloak of vapours,
Like a spirit seated on the throne of ages,
You raised the skies to your imperious face.

Pyramids of nature,
Peaks, summits, grandeur,
Whose gigantic structure
Speaks to man of his author;
Lofty mountains, undefined entity,
Depths and disharmony
That a propitious or deadly
Spirit sowed in these remote places;

Blood-red lightning flashes,
Dark cloud, eyrie from where the storm rushes
Leaping furious
Into the heart of the appalled heavens;
Gulfs, torrents, tempest, sea,
Carry me away in your horror!
For I love to feel the force of your
Wrath raging over me!
I love to contemplate your abysses,
Take measure of your high peaks,
Follow your sublime waves,
Be glutted with your terrors;
To constantly merge my essence
With winds, with flame, with waves,
For my heart is excited and rages
And everything inside me intensifies!...

BATS AT GRAND FOND

Tide swallows beach and even gentle breakers
push through from the reef over the lagoon
and darken the shore. The sun has left its cloud
and collapsed into a ruddy mess below the horizon.
We walk up the sandy passageway onto Avenue
Leconte de Lisle, and the pings of sonar catch
us at sharp angles, placing us in the depths
of Grand Fond, wings clicking to maintain
an illusion of invincibility; hunting mechanism.
Tim's first sighting of a bat. And there's no mistake.
The one signals many, a cloud outside meteorology –
storm warning or aftermath; a weather known to locals –
calling us out, to stand transfixed but insist that we
should move on, adjust our spiritual gain.

Ghostly as the claws of quick crabs on coral sand.
Evasive as *cabots sauteurs* on black volcanic rock.
Rectilinear as wooden pallets tossed-up on steep
beaches where no reef protects from the deeps.
Molosse bat? What *we* call 'freetailed bats'?
Likely, but there are also *Taphiens de Maurice*
and a cemetery by the sea, where prophets
and homeless men sleep by tombs, staring
out to Madagascar and Africa, over unfathomable
skies. Maybe these *are* Mauritian Tomb Bats?
We hurry home. Did you see any white
on their chests, I ask? I don't think so, Tim says,
but it was hard to tell as the last light went fast.

CABOTS SAUTEURS

Blennys, blemmes, skippy dogs.

Sun low in the west, the *cabots sauteurs*
do their collective sticky leaps on black rocks,
rocks and dogs absorbing the last rays of sun
through the hollows and curls of lean waves
washing the island, shipyards with each dog
a vessel to be blessed, slap of waves and flesh,
where vacationers slip into the coral emollient,
a boy clapping the waves to halt! as he's learnt
to bring local buses to the next stop, and washed-up
brain-coral inducing too much introspection
while the sea sounds deep inside the eyes,
cyclone season fading, and stray thoughts
awakening via *cabots sauteurs*' rock-hopping,
wet sparks in the back of the mind, less tentative
than some might think reading codes of basalt.

CATAMARAN WORKS TO ROUND POINTE DES AIGRETTES

Foundational rocks darkly foment,
jutting out to break a wider sea,
reef close and lagoon closed out,
sea urchins shucked by last night's
heavy swell, ruined by this paretic calm;
purple eviscerate quality of death,
black spines still potent on bleached
coral débris, chilling as joggers crush
shells to tidemarks, and all the while
a limp catamaran works to leave open sea,
overloaded with sunset passengers
drinking a dying sun, even the gentle
breeze fading away to leave them all
becalmed out from Pointe des Aigrettes.
Bristling sea urchins prowl deep beneath
the sailors' dangling feet, the sea dyed
bloody-black with the ink of *force majeure*,
all that was written out of their bodies;
darkness offering little buoyancy.

TROPICBIRDS

Here, on the island, it's the white-tailed
tropicbird, the *paille-en-queue,* with its straw
tail tillering updrafts of ravines, or pivoting
volcanic rock-faces. It resonates. But on a tiny,
flat atoll in the same ocean, I once saw red-tailed
tropicbirds, signature tails cutting sunsets,
papercuts in heavy clouds, the criss-cross
of bloodshot eyes. I am told they're here also –
nesting at the far reach of their domain –
but I doubt they'll show themselves. No flash.
No epiphanies. No past as bright as your future,
a redlining. But the white tails I see everywhere:
the slash where stone rises hot into colder air.
I lose the tone of whiteness to sunlight, and follow
its arrow west, witnessing its own will and testament,
quill to sign off and to affirm islands large
or infinitesimally small, maybe going under;
their ocean-tide's climb and descent.

THE SEA IS WILD TODAY AND THE NO SWIM SIGNS ARE UP EVERYWHERE

the sea is wild today and the no swim signs are up everywhere.
there's a dead quiet, an almost calm over the town
though the breeze drives at the cliff-faces, up ravines,
the Rasta prophet man is given a spliff from a car window
and stoned, collapses to a street corner to sing the day away.
you can't forget about 'the attack'. it's everywhere in the absence.
the deepest ocean is a short way off: out into the spray,
through three sets of waves, and you fall off the edge.
thin reefs stop nothing, the coral breaks easily.
big sharks cross from Australia to South Africa
dwell down there, working their routes, surfacing
to search the collision of sea and landfall. growing older.
movement triggers every sense they have. they act.
the sea is a flood of senses. blood is just a sign.
and now the blamers and the haters of nature
compound one death by wanting more.
the cullers blame the off-islanders,
they blame the 'nature lovers', they blame
the 'marine sanctuary'. they blame blame blame
while a mother with baby daughter
empties what's left of her honeymoon
into the porous volcanic rock
which takes all water: fresh, salt, of the body . . .
where it flows down into the sea
where it all ends before space takes us all.

LA MER CASSÉE

Sugarcane on the verge
of harvest slices the light
to thin bone. It rustles
sharply on slopes, its juice
the heart of commerce
though tamarind
cools the island.

And where ocean
breaks even the toughest
volcanic rocks, a black & white
world of old photos
surges up to pandanus
and casuarinas gripping
knuckled earth.

Chitons grip hard
to make their living.

I KNEW THIS PATH THROUGH CYPRESSES, AN OLIVE-GROVE

I knew this path through cypresses, an olive-grove;
I'd followed it repeatedly and waved away
The pine-needle cobwebs from my face, to see
Between the cypresses that blue glimpse of the bay –

The little bay that opens out invitingly,
The little beach where locals take their ease.
I was in love with everything I saw:
The olive-leaves that shimmied in the slightest breeze,

The donkey groaning under its hump of straw;
The little bar, the dry clicking noises made
By worry beads in the fingers of old men
Who sat to *tavli* at wooden tables in the shade,

The fried fish and the wine full of resin, then;
With the opalescent blue-greens of the water
And with the mermaid who swam in on the tide
And parted salt-wet lips as her mother taught her

And slicked herself before she slid me inside;
With her grey-green eyes, their fleck like foam
On a choppy sea, and how they opened wide
As she rocked above me in that hidden cove.

I can still hear that clicking metronome,
Can hear small waves collapsing up the shore;
I can see the birthmark, a tiny a patch of home
Above her tail, where I'd made landfall long before...

THE BOURBON BAUDELAIRE

(i) Out of 'Parfum exotique'

Closed-eye crepuscular,
Scent realising breasts
Covered or free, yielding
Landfall bedazzling fiery
Overbearing sun, somnambulist isle,
Nature proffering singular trees
And luscious fruits, ripping six-packs
And undressing eyes but not intrusive;
Nose to your odour, fermenting,
Chanting *climate*, lagoon and sandfall,
Masts clinking, worn to the bones
Of wrecking waves on black rocks,
Green-fanned perfume swishing air,
Swells and bloods my soul in its lair.

(ii) Out of 'A une malabaraise'

Delicate hands and feet and broad-hipped
To induce envy in the whitest of women;
Love to indulge over and above your body.
Your rebel eyes, black skin exchange
Lost to blue hands where your God caused
Your birth; light the master's pipe to funeral
Stands of chilled water and scents
To drive away the roaming mosquitoes
And plain trees aubade sumptuous
Pineapples and bananas at the bazaar –
For the overlord – lifting one exposed foot
After the other; hum low old ditties

We don't know. Scarlet-decked sunset,
Natte of supple body to let dreams
Float *colibris* and eternally as yourself
Gracious and blooming: resplendent.
Why child do you want the hexagon
And its anachronising, that bloated country
Scythed by suffering, giving body and soul
To the muscled sailors, ardour adieu, tamarinds
(rhymes with sailors, so why not?), you
Semi-naked in fragile muslins shivering
In that cold clime (snow, hail), you'd weep
For sweet pleasures if locked in by a corset,
Dragging supper out of muddy streets,
To sell your scented 'charms' – pensive
Voyage through gas-fogs, the spectres
Of your coconut palms.

(iii) Out of 'La Vie antérieure'

Long-lived beneath vast porticoes
Tint of sun on ocean times one thousand burnings,
O great columns arrow straight, regal,
Resembling in construct caves of basalt evenings.

Image-swollen skies roll
Concealing something mystically
Almighty cloud-music overloading
Sunset colours reflected in my gaze;

That's where I dwelled in calm sensuality,
Content in azure, waves' splendours,
Naked slaves who will – *must* –
Get permeated with aromas, the scent of evil;

Who cooled my palms, knows,
So for shallow caves deepening
Painful secret of my languishing.
Who gets the raw deal here?

(iv) Out of 'La Chevelure'

Lamb-fleece ripple collar!
O nonchalant perfume
Ecstatic peopled orderly alcove
Asleep in head of hair to shake out.

Languorous Asia, Burning Africa,
Distance absent almost dead
Aromatic forest as other minds seek music
I swim on for perfume.

I will go under tree sap and name
Something in parrot's chattering desire,
The canopy of beach umbrella shadow,
Starving sea dazzling nightmare souls and their masts.

Elongating export wealth, past sensual drinks
To satisfy the yearning western urge,
Gliding vessels on silken waters open vastly
The glory of continental drift in shark lanes.

Eternity trembles outside whirlwind's
Head-plunge, drunken lust, black ocean
Black sails othering me, patch of canvas
Rocking and craving leisure-domes – Blue Hair!

Pavilion-stretched shadows return azure
Immense globular sky of velvet edges
Of locks twisted on coconut mats and spires,
Hand in your mane, scattering

Rubies, pearls and sapphires
So that you're never dead to my desire
O ominous dream? Or not? The ground
I guzzle memory from?

IN MY NEW LIFE I AM THE SKIPPER

In my new life I am the skipper
Of an old tramp steamer that plies the trade routes
Between Southampton and the River Plate, or
Feels its way rustily along the Equator.
While she is stuck with a premature ejaculator
Who never waits for her to come before he shoots.

In my new life I build my eyrie
High above the jungle, where the parrots cry
And take my pleasure at sundown on the verandah
With rum and glistening girls, one blue of eye,
One brown; while his tongue grows weary
In her suburban bed, and she wishes he would die.

In my new life we croon together,
Lascars, girls and I, a sweet Hawaiian air
While she spends her afternoons and evenings where
The unschooled, rising raucous voices gather
To celebrate the marriage of punishing heat
And barbecues and beer and bleeding meat.

In my new life I have three children –
Three faces in which I see her face, her eyes
The colour of the deep green water off Sardinia;
Beautiful as she is in their freckled skins.
Two boys and a girl. They run races –
The boys are skinnier, but she always wins.

PASSAGE THROUGH ICEBERGS (PAINTED AS *VOYAGE TO LABRADOR* BY ALFRED WALLIS, 1935–6)

Pinnacles accompanying steady
Course, the odd dry-docked
Whiteness with its blue-ice seams,
The odd growler knocking oxygen
Out of the hull as we steam luminous
Waters locked into night.

Sudden crash of calving mother
Itself calved from a Greenland glacier,
Rollover to drift haphazardly or
Just play random, notched at plimsoll,
Swelling headstrong below
Solid guesswork. You dreamt

Mantras and narratives
Of Arthur Gordon Pym, pole
Switching, high-risk passage,
Lovecraft's *Mountains of Madness*
Hemisphering a bloody swirl
In beckoning hydrodynamics;

Or the reactor at McMurdo
Shelling out its 'atoms for peace'.
But north again and windward
Of shadows and their dark lien,
Nautilus under the sheets
Or on the skin of Greenland

At North Star Bay, a fallen
Warhead drilling down down
And vanishing. On the ship's bent decks
Where perspective fails in fallout,
We hear a sailor's call resound:
'And the sun did shine so cold'.

LOG

The maelstrom! Could a more dreadful word in a more dreadful situation have sounded in our ears! . . . From every point of the horizon enormous waves were meeting, forming a gulf justly called 'The Navel of the Ocean', whose power of attraction extends to a distance of twelve miles. There, not only vessels, but whales are sacrificed, as well as white bears from the northern regions.
– *Jules Verne,* Twenty Thousand Leagues Under the Sea

Myself, Fairford and the boy, deckhands on the *Scarface*
(Nantucket) huddled by Buxton, who took the wheel,
And Captain George Currie – and Jenkins, gnawing a frost-bitten sole,
Turns to us his fat white moustache of frost and ice,
Fluffy-looking, like a kid all stuck with candy-floss
Or ice-cream from a cornet – but with something of his dad's
Who was in whalers before him (*his* dad remembered the days of sail).
At first he'd laughed, called it *the rime of the ancient mariners,*
But now he fixed us with a glinting eye, shouted *Steady lads!*
This here's the maelstrom, the navel of the ocean! –
Sort of barmy voice. We thought he'd begun to rave
But scraped off white stars from the ports of the deckhouse
And saw, miles around, from every point of the horizon,
Running towards the gulf, enormous wave on wave...

It was weeks since we'd lost sight of the fleet – seen only pack-ice
Drifting farther and farther south, and not a single whale,
Not a single living thing, neither sea-bird nor seal;
Then yesterday, early morning watch, Soutar cried out twice:
Fuckin' Christ man there's bears on it, and peering under the fleece
Of our hoods we could see them moving, outlines, shadows,
White on whiter white; and terror stabbed each soul
At how long we'd been steaming north. We stood like mourners

As Cladd ran fo'ard, fired; watched the spirit that was Cladd's
Explode out of him in a white cloud, a frosty exhalation.
Chedglow chipped him off of the gun with an ice-pick;
We boiled and ate most of him, stewed with scurvy-cress,
Stowed the leftovers, the dainties, which were instantly frozen.
Last night I dreamt of dressed fingers, toes in aspic,

And today we saw the bear we'd skewered – one more sacrifice,
Crumpled, wasted...A moment later we hit the swell,
White swirls, foam plunging, *Each wave swallowin' itsel'*
Soutar screamed, and we were drawn in, down, but not to green-white peace;
For there alongside us, as we sank further from the floes,
Swam a multitude of dead or dying things: otters, gulls, their eyelids
Clogged shut, their fur and feathers claggy with effluents, oil;
Among the whaling-boats, trawlers, ketches, catamarans
We saw blood-spattered seals, tunny trailing swim-bladders;
Whales spewing pink froth, each stuck like a huge pin-cushion
With harpoons; pocked, distended creatures, as from a blasted ark –
All this I begged Jenkins to set down, not to secure for us
Pardon, still less Larsen's fame, but so that we might keep our reason
Should we come back alive out of this deep cold, this dark.

CARRAIGLEA AUBADE

The essential parts of the world are outlines –
slivers of existence where light meets obstacle,
where reflection and absorbency reveal
more than any life-sapping collider.
The slice of slate at eighty degrees
at first light makes shadows
deeper than the smallest particle,
the obsession of a denuding age.
The sea isn't a mirror, that red herring,
but a barrier that pings sight
and exclamations, the indrawn
breath denoting beauty,
sends them back to their makers,
so full of love and lust,
and anxious anticipation
of an implacable sun.

LONG AFTER (*JEAN GENET*)

That purple anemone, that shit-streaked whorl,
Its dark pink heart seeping semen-pearls,
Its hairs as neat, as silky as a girl's,
That offers both salvation and the Fall;
A compact has been worked out between
It, or your mouth, and this other guy's cock:
A fisherman of eighteen or nineteen
In blue shorts – and always hard as a rock.

At night he comes to you out of the blue,
The white houses, six sullen dead girls' heads
Strung on his belt, in a stink of sea-beds;
The hot shame his hard-on kindles in you
Can only be put out by his spurt and splash
Of spunk. *No, don't go yet.* But he pulls away
And darkness fills you; on his lip a slash
Of white foam, in his eyes a mist of spray . . .

So you lie alone, forgotten by him when
He's out cold, his head in the crook of your arm.
He sleeps. You dare not move. The sea is calm.
If he should wake and look at you – what then?
What if – worse than his leaving you in dreams –
He threw up on your tits? Would you pick through
The wine and meat and bile, the purple streams
And bits of pink, his only ties to you?

CARRAIGLEA

We could perch on the grey rock
overlooking a slated cove
on Long Island Channel
where clots of seaweed
are worked by long-legged
sea birds, and skuas alter
the wind's direction with sheer
willpower, affecting the weather
patterns of the great Atlantic Ocean;
where otters came in before
building work drove them away,
where a single old seal cruises
out of Schull Harbour, past
the deep-pitted cemetery
with its thousands,
past Schull Point,
all the navigation markers
and lights of 'warding-off'
and 'rounding' suck in daylight
to sustain their hope through nights,
where a whale was sighted
and where a famous novel
was written and PhDs completed,
and where we might cram together
and look out through windows
large as shelter, as hungry
for calm and action
as any sailor or poet
might want.

SPREE

All the wines have gone away
To the sunshine and the sea,
Whisky, bitter, gone to stay
In the mountains, where they're free;
Gin and absinthe, those slow killers,
Left their dark Victorian villas
And the pub, the old Green Pillars –
Gone on their annual spree!

Feel the fine salt drizzle falling
On the undercliff's red clay,
Hear the gulls like drowned souls calling
To be saved on judgement day;
Feel your fifty years, a cargo
To make your aching timbers groan;
Sharks have placed under embargo
Everything you called your own.

Now a panicked hue and cry
Goes up from the gulls that wheel
Through a massive slate-grey sky
Above me, where I stand and reel;
Here, the thistled, grass-grown clifftop;
Down below, the slate-grey, stiff chop
Of the sea; should I – what if? – drop,
Would that make this more *real*?

OUT OF THE COTTAGE'S BIG FEATURE WINDOWS

The early warning signs: kittywakes, silver gulls, shearwaters, petrels.
The boat coming to hook ropes beneath fluorescent orange buoys.
They could have been seals at dawn, but aren't, and will never
be so for us again. What would the amateur artist who summered
here year after year, decade after decade, make of this? Water-colours.
The boatman hauls his traps and hurls the dead and unwanted corpses
out onto the surface, to be picked by the birds. The windows
of this place drink it in and make moving pictures
of our distress. The projector shakes with the camera's
tentative images, moving with jerks and a Saint Vitus dance
charge. It's a silent movie and shows little mercy,
the nitrate film volatile and shiny as the water
slicking its way between the Head and Long Island
where the man will sail on to sort and ice his kill.
A heron lands on rocks to examine where he had been.

SHIP OF FOOLS

How were they led to water, to chartering the leaky boat –
Old twin-berth, twelve knots, no mast or sail, no swivel chair:
Less than what you'd want, say, for a week-end's pottering around
In a tributary of the Teme, where you *could* run aground,
Drop anchor in a kiddies' paddling pool, or scare
A shoal of minnows, or capsize a boy's bobbing float –
Young men who in their daily lives oozed *savoir faire*,

Even under pressure, always knowing what was what?
Rescue them, can't we, from whatever brought them here,
South of everything they knew, to chance a fishing trip, a
Brothel and a salty bar, a boat without a skipper;
Opened them to influences of the tropics; showed them fear;
Amazed two stomachs shrivelled tightly to a single knot,
Then burst their lungs with blackness? No, it's written in the plot,

In the stars they could not read, in the pride their natures felt
Shrugging off the obstacles to things they chose to do,
Forcing all the world to grant their every slightest wish,
On the cutting edge of options, in the blind pursuit of fish;
United on this point, that whatsoever they projected, few –
No-one, that's to say – objected to. No deal undealt,
Dirty trick untried, no shit unheaped on someone's dish…

* * *

They had drifted half a world from Cape Halfalump
While one of them tried to coax the fuel pump
Or untangle the screw, the rudder-thing, and the other sot
Made a meal of fish-heads and blood-smells and sat
Entranced by the click-click of his ratchet and his line
Nonchalantly winking in the sun. Then they were alone,
Massively, with the fish for company and something brewing

In the sky like a wet bruise, the slap of waves, the boat slewing
Sideways on to them, tiny, slung between two green-mauve
Spires of a great sea-cathedral that was on the move.
Imagining the worst (and some imaginings are true),
Not knowing yet what it would be, they went below to try
Getting through with *Mayday* or an SOS – the radio-ham thing –
But neither of them knew how to work the damn thing.

Every hour that went by took them further from help;
Lower and lower came the sky, the sea rose like an Alp;
In no time their few supplies were washed, yo-ho-ho,
Easily overboard, merrily bobbing as water sloshed, yo-ho, o-
Ver the gunwhale, round the deck and back to its, yo-ho, h-
Eaving, sliding lair. At last it was still, but no-one cried *Ahoy!*;
Dead calm, empty, flat horizon. Days. *Swim for it.*

* * *

Did they know, now, what was coming, and did they fear it?
Rudderless, the decks and paintwork blistered, cracked;
Outboard flooded: thus the boat was found, with seven crooked
Weals scratched in the fibreglass, no fishing gear,
No clothes, nothing, not a trace or Garth or Greer
Except for hanks of their hair – they had tied hooks to these,
Dangled them, watch fish take them and break them with ease.

CHARTER

To read surface is to read depth and tide,
the rushing in and rushing out, the sibilant
emptying and refilling, the slick where stillness
over channels compliments weedy shallows,
where the breeze through islands makes
the glassy sheen of staring too hard into origins,
coming out of the sea to occupy land.
Slicks of high tide confuse patches of oil
from trawlers and smaller boats, but they
don't show on charts and are denied
as local knowledge explains each slick,
each tone of the sea, each texture,
the rainbow films in rockpools
denied or cast as restricted phenomena,
the subfusc light denying until sun-up.

YARAVI

(after Valery Larbaud)

In this great blast of black wind that we plough through
Exalted, tearful, I walk up and down the bridge of the yacht;
Midnight at sea, and no land in sight.
Just a while ago, as the sun went down,
In the fog, the cannon of the Bosphorus were rumbling,
The Asian side replying to the European side
(A guide to shipping), on the quarter-hour.
And it was with this warlike commotion astern
That my boat, so drolly named the *Narrenschiff*
Plunged into pitch-black night and chaos on the Black Sea…

A child again, I scoured that darkness
Where we made headway,
Where the great porphyry waves rolled in
Freighted with livid flowers of sea-edelweiss.

Tomorrow! Day breaking on the coast
And on my heart, full of bells!
Stretching to infinity, the shores of the Ottoman Empire
In gentle undulations of pink and green
Where earth-coloured villages and old fortresses lie hidden;
Or the entrance to a Russian port, announced
By thousands of green gourds bobbing on the sparkling water
As Ausonia sometimes, more discreetly, announces itself
To the seafarer with a little empty wine-bottle, raffia-covered,
Rocked by the Tyrrhenian swell…

Oh, the summer sunrises on the ringing waters
And the silence of coastlines seen from afar!

But let me get a little sentimental about my childhood,
Let me see myself again, at fifteen, in the streets of Odessa;

Let me weep in the night without knowing why
And declaim those lines into the wind,
'Ya que para mi no vives'
To a waltz tune heard I don't know where, a Gipsy tune,
Let me sing through my sobs, to a Gipsy tune!
Memory shows me again some dazzling landfalls:
The sea-roads full of shipping and the blue harbours
Edged by quaysides planted with giant palms and colossal
Fig-trees, like leather awnings suspended from the sky;
And vast half-submerged forests,
And the shadowy *paseos* of Barcelona;
Silver and cut-glass domes deep in the azure
And Antikythera, hollowed like a champagne glass,
Where, beside the most peaceful streams in the world,
All the ancient pastorals are performed;
And those Greek islands floating in the sea....

Is it joy or despair that makes me weep so, mixing
My stifled sobs with the panicky shrieking of the gale,
With the rhythm of the engine-room, the thunder, and the hissing
Of the waves' glassy mass that twists
Along the sides of the boat and lets go suddenly,
Spread like a cloak of precious stones
(But none of this can be seen...)

But my sadness...Oh, my beloved sadness!
Who will take on this groundless sadness,
Which the past didn't know, whose secret the future
Will doubtless not know either?
Oh, to prolong the memory of this modern sadness,
This sadness which has no cause, but which
Is a gift from heaven.

WRECKED SPANISH GALLEON AND VESTIGIAL PROPERTY AND IDENTITY ANXIETIES

It's darkening, and the sea exposes
rocks and clots of carrageen, an out-

turning or phase shift we acclimatise
as tidal. Not far out from this point

a Spanish galleon, wreck of Apocrypha –
I was always called 'Black Irish'

in my Anglophile primary school
locked into swampy land of the Swan

Coastal Plain. 'Black Irish' because
Armada sailors had fertilised local

girls along the Irish coast. But then
my clan with its 'foul laughter'

were inland on flattish country
and then foresters up the mountains

of Wicklow. The black blood flowing
inwards and upwards. Tracy wonders

if in fact it *is* just rocks and seaweed
or something else (maybe otters returning),

and I say I'll walk down and check,
drizzle making its sheen of the black rocks

and the navigation lights already bright
like a light opera, maybe *Pirates of Penzance*,

or like the wicked fishing boat, that empties
the bay of life, being a magnet for seabirds,

a Pig Pen to the flies, or even like that long
spooky vessel with its outboard that putters

into the lagoon of *Gilligan's Island*.
Now I'm in the John Ashbery poem (how

many claims for this state of mind
are made?), but that doesn't detract

from any of the questions I am working
over moving closer to the rocks and lapping

water, the revelations of retreating tide.
But I am to be stretched further still

in the competing imagery, the anxiety
of conflicting and competing thoughts:

I come across a half-eaten apple and the 'cooked'
shell of a crustacean. Who has been on 'our'

shoreline, shore cut off from elsewhere
other than by long drive past Carraiglea

or landing furtively by boat. No curtains close
the massive window we survey the bay from,

and privacy is isolation. Not believing
in private property (our rights of rental),

I am caught. But privacy is not property,
and the rights of acknowledgement

come into play. When that galleon
went down, those rocks played

their ambiguities, and my 'darker
skin' sourced from Ireland in the mid-

nineteenth century (I am told) plays
the light for all it's worth. I don't believe

any of it: my being here, the strangers'...
the intruders'... picnic (or do locals

change such rules?); that deadly boat
plucking fish from where dead sailors

rest, where survivors bend national
identities to be denied.

LOST

Every year,
Ships disappear;
Pass over a horizon
No-one has his eyes on
And into history,
Into a mystery,

Aerials humming,
Power lines down;
The floating wealth
Nowhere under the sun.
How can a man drown
And not see it coming?

A matter of stealth
And the waters have won –
A shoal, a cliff,
A rock, a reef,
Your Narrenschiff
Has come to grief –

Your ship of fools
Now resting on
That sandy bed
Where only schools
Of flitting fish
Have traffic with

The quiet dark,
Shoot past glowing
Ranks of dials –
One still showing
Full steam ahead –
And clean-picked smiles,

The lips long gone;
The treasure-hoard
Lost beyond reach
Of tycoon, warlord,
Speculating leech
And cruising shark.

FIGUREHEAD OF THE CLIPPER *SAMUEL PLIMSOLL*

(sunk after collision with the *Dalgoma* at Gage Road, Fremantle, 1948)

Long after life, long in the tooth, wood-
          wormed and out of time,
stripped from the hulk as was the fashion,
          barely seaworthy, towed
from Adelaide to Fremantle stored in a cabin,
          figurehead of the *Samuel Plimsoll*
resting in its coffin ship. We might think
          Plimsoll himself rises here,
determinedly placid, proud to have been
          a champion of the poor,
elevated to the order of maritime angels
          (secular and superstitious,
religious and non-denominational).
          Doesn't modernity begin
in part, with this effigy shaking
          a fist at Disraeli,
with wrecks and deaths littering shores
          and the ocean floor,
drawing a line in the sand, a tidal mark
          we hope won't be breached?
But it is. Safety knows its limits, floats
          to the level of profit
and loss. Clipper ships sail museum seas,
          and coal hulks haunt
ports large and small, clinging on
          against the breeze
that would have taken them out to sea lanes,
          to the surging deeps.
Mounted on the wall, a wooden draft,
          a fixed freeboard
to comfort him, though no rise and fall
          of swell to vary his view,

shake his stare, and no saltwater
to break down his colours;
only the seawinds at stone walls, rattling
windows. Hauled up
from the wreck, shouting from the cabin
of the desecrated hull,
making ripples we can still see as we stare
down from wharves,
from the sides of enormous steel ships,
as the harbour writhes
with 'live export': sheep working buoyancy,
dead clouds on the water,
figureheads that will leave no trace.

LONG AFTER (*EUARISTOS KALFAS*)

O the beautiful head of that dutiful daughter
In the prow of the boat that plied between islands,
Between one and another hot-shaded silence –
She took along the parasol her mother bought her
That was like a little piece of home, her home:
A suburban garden, parakeets, galahs...
(I hear the wet *click-click* of the metronome
Her body made, working me; shattered compass-glass
Shows my course veering drunkenly, true South to
Magnetic North, from rage to love and back to rage,
The calmer latitudes I hoped would come with age
Had vanished, while that salt source I put my mouth to
Tasted brackish, bitter...) Still dripping water
She lay propped on the elbow of one freckled arm;
I watched the shadow of her parasol grow shorter
On the deck – onshore, a Cubist village, single palm,
A beach festooned with nets, all trembling at high noon
When sunlight struck them...A jug of local wine
In the shade of that palm, and a twisting vine,
And the shuttered cool we rented for the afternoon!

EMPTIED VESSEL

The bay has been emptied,
a dirty ring on the bath
revealed. The oil slick we
watched in its line across
the harbour mouth, woven
through the hundred islands,
a sheen on ocean's plastic,
dispersed. Though in twilight,
the oil film left on pools trapped
in their rocky footholds, menisci
on lips of erosion's threshold,
to give to slipways, smooth
as defiance which is no more
than collusion, nearby. The
tide telling blatant truisms.
A gentle, rhetorical wave,
then spilling over rocks, slipping
onto shingle and broken shells,
and I am surprised by childhood.
My brother and I working over
rockpools, our tensions
and excitements, our oneness.
Those who would call it nostalgia
might do so because they fear
or lack. Such reimaging pushes
back the pollution, makes you
stand your ground, realise
you're barely oceans apart.

ANOINTED, SWEAT-STREAKED, REDDENED, RAW

Anointed, sweat-streaked, reddened, raw
We turned our backs to the sea's great rosy flush.
The sun had gone to live behind the mountain;
The mountain had changed colour – so had she,
Propped on her elbow while I towelled my gooseflesh.

One day, the excavator's giant claw
Ploughed a furrow out of shingle, fish-heads, shells –
Dislodging one smell made of many smells.
The square gave up its table, benches, fountain;
Four times an hour, the church bell tolled *for thee*...

The village was all white stone houses, stairs.
The fishing boats slept all night under the stars
And far out where the sky and water met
A giant lizard's back had risen from the sea.
When I touched that dutiful daughter, she was wet...

FULL MOON OVER LONG ISLAND BAY

The moon is frighteningly close.
Things are going to be pulled apart.
Tim is watching a DVD about meteor
impacts and is worried about Apophis
but we tell him it has already passed.
This doesn't alleviate the tension.
The moon sucks at the bay
and we can see the water
curl towards impact craters.
I have the binoculars out and give
a running report. The bay will undergo
a name change and people will forget
what it was like before this event.
And I am not the same person
writing this minutes later,
taken away by the eyes,
my old self, already changeling,
welded to glass, the moon, the bay.

I WAS IN IRONS. THE BULKHEADS GROANED; AND THEN A LULL

I was in irons. The bulkheads groaned; and then a lull,
The slopping of the sea, the steady beat and thresh
Of wings, and again the unforgiving cry of that gull
Came through the small hushed waves' repeated fresh

Collapse among the rock-pools of the shallows;
I knew the face that bobbed before me in the updraft
And beckoned me towards the cockpit, but when I went aft
The bird still flapped and flew around my head: 'Aloes.

A little something for the weekend. Ambre Solaire.
Jojoba. Such were the unguents that you'd apply
To salve each other's arms and legs and backs, cooked rare
To medium: *Life's a beach, and then you die* –

Remember that? And the hot night trains through Europe
To Liguria's green bays? You were no sightseer
But on a poet's pilgrimage: Rapallo, Sestri's Via
Byron and the Bay of Silence where she threw up

At the sight of a grilled fish served whole on her plate....
Remember the bikini slipping off her breast
In Leghorn – the salt taste of her, still wet, as you ate –
Where they plucked out Shelley's heart and burned the rest?

Remember scenes and tears, and learning your three Rs –
Remorse, regret, recrimination – and the time she took
To come, and how you put the whole thing in a book
And told the world how much you loved her pretty arse?

Half of your life you've been your own worst enemy
And now you taste another one's seaweed and salt
And lie awake at night asking if it was your fault
And take it out on her and her little sea-anemone…

Have you no shame? Put away your rank jottings from
Some provincial Don Juan's boudoir, and refrain
From scratching at old sores. These rocks, this beach, this prom,
These breakwaters lashed by English waves, by English rain

Will always call you back. What could better anchor you
To work and memory, the permanence of loss?
I know what's on your one-track mind, you wanker you –
I, your duty, your conscience and your albatross!'

ALBATROSS

(after Baudelaire)

Just to amuse themselves, deckhands will often take
A great sea-bird, an albatross –
One of those that plane above the ship's white wake
As it pitches over briny chasms, shipwrecks, dross.

No sooner have they plonked it on the deck, those boors
Than the lord of deep blue air, as if shamed,
Lets its huge wings droop like oars
To trail beside it, self-conscious, maimed.

How clumsy and useless he is, who was so noble,
A moment ago; how comical and vile,
The winged voyager! One old salt sticks a pipe in his bill;
Another mimics him, limping, cripple-style.

The Poet is a lot like this prince of the clouds,
Who haunts the storm, and mocks the archer taking aim;
On earth, exiled among the jeering crowds,
It's his own great wings that make him lame.

SELKIES LASHING THE ROCKS

Waves break over the rocks slanting
north-east, the coast leaning towards
glaciers as if they're about to return,
a wishful thinking as it warms
and the small fish in the marshy pool
are charged with the breakers fizzing
at the edges, intense aeration where
navigation is constant and bloody.
Those domes on the rock – their art
and worship – the salt-white beacons
on headlands, the pulsing lights
to warn of rocks, moraines where cold
once slew the spirit, rode on horses
out of the ocean and took warm-blooded
men deep below the icebergs of the past.

WILD

Raging over rocks
Sea opens anemones:
Wild snakelocks, beadlets.

I KNEW THIS PATH, THE PROMENADE, THE LANES

I knew this path, the promenade, the lanes,
The old Refreshment Room, closed-down First Aid Post,
The lichen-growing walls, the salt insistent rains –
'Refreshment or First Aid, which do you need most?

Half your life on the sea-floor, and now you're back
To walk below the wet clay of the undercliff
Like a dripping cistern, wade through bladderwrack,
Through brittle crab-claws, starfish bleached and stiff!...'

I knew this path – how it hurt to remember –
Across the marsh to dunes and marram grass,
To the sea, to miles of empty sand at Camber
Where she tucked her skirt up round her thighs, her arse

And waded in; the little stagnant lough,
The gulls' and high-stepping waders' curving strand.
'Gull-cries follow you towards the point, cut off
On three sides, where you have to take yourself in hand

As that wave breaks over you, goes back out
And leaves you beached and retching for air,
And sea and sky and solid ground in doubt –
Skirt bunched, laughing, wading in: *she is not there...*'

THE PRAGMATISM OF INLAND BIRDS

Jackdaws and ravens have been flying
down from mountains with apples
plucked small from orchards to drop
onto coastal rocks, smashing fruit
on black outcrops, a red blush, succulent
interior, pips that will fall into sea
like a demigod's tears.

Jackdaws and ravens have been flying
down from mountains with apples
to smash as oyster-catchers are smashing
mussels plucked from the bay, bodies
turned inside out and pincered
by red beaks. A peripatetic crow
witnessed and reported back.

MUTE SWANS OVER CARRAIGLEA

Four with their white wings
'wheezing' a refrain, following
the black coastline. All life
lifts to their passing.

Seeing them is not dependent
on eyesight, sensing their musical
flight not dependent on hearing.
Each wingsweep bridges silence.

The leader flies higher and the others
stack below to step down so the first
is last, the second, third.
Harmonics are also involved.

All life knows this more than
its own sentience. All inanimate
presence shudders under the force.
Rocks shimmer, Carraiglea shudders.

SHARKS

(Film-poem)

Over the whole long day, the shimmering water,
Over the diesel-stench, the thrumming screw,
Over the sudden sense that life could fail
To be that richer riskier thing I knew
Before the years of drift, in the days of sail –
I draw a veil of flapping canvas, salt and air
That danced and wavered with petroleum,
That was not fit to breathe, that was as thick as glair…
We lay off Sardinia – no dockside mooring
But a little bay in which we rode at anchor
While the moving cliff-side of a super-tanker,
Rust-streaked behind its oil-rich haze of heat
Steamed by. I had blagged my way here as crew
On a mystery Russian's super-yacht,
Hardly any smaller – this was before the crash,
Not that the crash would have bothered *him*:
He had made himself a billionaire
By dealing in dismay, and wanted to atone
By bankrolling lost-cause arts (this poem,
Say). A super-model and some forty matelots
On board too. She sprawled on sun-deck pillows,
His starlet, in the scrap of scarlet scrim
That failed to hide her neat, gym-hardened rear –
After lunch, I'd watched her squirm and shriek
As, full of grappa, grappling with it, he
Succeeded in exposing one small cheek –
And seemed to be inviting one of us to eat
With a look that acknowledged frankly how *boring*
That would be…

                    I missed the dutiful daughter
Who only felt at home this far from home,
Which made me think of other berths I'd known:

In Blackfriars I'd survived the plumbing of my fears
As grappling hooks with heavy lines were thrown
About me, and I felt my timbers groan;
In Clerkenwell, hard by the unreal City
I learned their lessons, it was sink or swim
In the brown swirling current of careers,
No quarter given, no place for fear or pity
Below decks or above; in the cork-hung bars
On the south coast, among the salt-edged cries
Of gulls, I was gifted seven spendthrift years
Which I spent falling face-down in a ditch
One eye on the taproom clock, one on the stars.
And I recalled that greenish wharf in Greenwich,
Domes and spires, and crane-reflecting water
And friends I saw as through a veil of tears,
Their smiles wiped from their faces by a flood
Of griefs, the soaking of their dry hard wit
And the whole bloody issue covered in mud;
And in New York, in a bar down by the piers
Where I sat drinking bourbons chased by beers
I'd kept company with a one-eyed, soused old salt
Who had sailed with Melville – such, anyway, was
His drunken boast. (He had known some drunken boats:
Compass shattered, mainsail torn to shreds,
The bo'sun with the ship's grog ration in the heads,
The skipper and first mate at each other's throats.)
And in Wapping our cruiser, with a crew from Oz,
Came under fire; was holed on the starboard bow,
The ship's log gone overboard, the ratings drowned –
I crouched in the foc's'le, stubbly to a fault,
Bailing for all I was worth…
                                        I came round
From this daydream, glanced into the drugged eyes
Of Anastasia, and went down below –
What I would have given for a bit of blow

Myself, or failing that a tot of rum.
At the galley porthole, jabbing its huge beak
Against the glass, my gull-familiar squawked:
There's never been a bunk you haven't walked
(Or crawled) away from, looking foolish, weak;
And now by divers courses you have come
On this unnatural berth, maybe your last.
Your nights are all bad dreams soaked in remorse,
Your days all lost in longing for what's past
And past repair, for that life on the ocean wave
You never led, the unknown, uncharted course
In your head, for what lies beyond, beyond…
Instead you must drudge and cark and care
For worldly trash; you have no offshore haven
Full of guilt-edged bonds, no fortress-hideaway
Built by your unearned cash, and graven
On your tired heart are the words: Work and Die.
Meanwhile, they've taken everything you love
(With a twist of its head it indicated Nikolai,
Whose jet-ski buzzed and buffeted the billows)
And debauched it, left it debased, in hock
To money. An iron fist in a black silk glove,
Diamond-studded, unthinking as that blonde
Has gripped the world of living things and all
Its wealth of beauty – such as this coast, those
Purple-tinted hills, those vines and olive groves;
This deep blue air and pinkish-white sea-floor
And, between, the element that keeps you afloat,
That teems with fish, food of both rich and poor
Alike, for centuries – but for how long now?
Whatever they can't turn to profit or
To power, they turn to shit – that is their way.
Soon there'll be nowhere left to walk or crawl
Or swim, nowhere to sink in but the gutter;
What you believed will seem the saddest song,

The truths you trusted gone, unwanted, wrong,
As much protection as an old tweed coat
Against the surge, the flood-tide of schlock
And sticky effluent, desire and greed
That rises higher, stinking worse each day.
You are for feeding on, while I live to feed...
He flapped off, whereon I heard the stutter
And cough of an engine throttled back –
Our master-mariner now leapt aboard.
It seemed I was not the only one who'd heard
The diatribe of that most truculent bird,
For within moments a mutinous gang
Had gathered by the gangway, seized their prey,
Tied him up with taunts and blows, keel-hauled him
And thrown him over, lashed to the stern-post,
Bleeding, pleading for his life – they called him
'Parasite', 'gob-shite' and 'shark-meat', sang
Profane sea-shanties and the 'Internationale';
Then some, casting off and steaming full ahead
Steered for the open sea, dragging sternmost
The bloody stump that screamed out (not quite dead)
As more was bitten off at each attack –
While others, no doubt with their own rationale,
Turned their thoughts to her they called 'the broad'...

[*To be contd.*]

LOT'S WIFE

She stands fifty foot over Baltimore
And looks out onto the wrecks in the Bay.
Given her lot, would you expect her to care?
'Beacon' is hardly a name to inspire confidence
Despite standing so tall and white and brash
For all sailing towards the rocks to see.

MERMAID (*THE SAILOR'S MEMORY*)

Gone, now, the masts, the hiss and roar of surf, the foam,
Gone the swell, the shingle and the smell of kelp,
The whine in the rigging, the sea-howl and sea-yelp
And everything you loved when far from home.

Gone the grey stone sea-wall and the jaunty harbour
Where you watched the pennants flapping and the furled
Sails ruffled by a breeze from half-way round the world,
Gone the jetty and the vine-leaf-shaded arbour

Where you sat in a daze of leave-taking and tears;
Gone the galleys, the caiques and the triremes
And all the wrecked and drowned armadas of your dreams,
The song the sirens sang, the music of the spheres.

Gone the tides, the wave-ridged, gull-flecked, glistening sand,
The greenish wood at waterline, the oil you spilt,
The slicked birds and slimed fish; the dark mud-stink of guilt
That clung to you, the drowned man's hand that clutched your hand.

Gone the life unlived, the coasts unseen, uncharted.
Gone, almost, your own sad heart that slobbers on the poop,
Your heart all black-tobacco-blue; gone the awful soup
They chucked at it, and the captains long departed.

Gone the cries of Jack Tars, and their ithyphallic
Brutish jokes, and the jets and gobs their frigging in
The rigging drenched you with; gone the ships' boys' moleskin
Breeches, tight-packed, and the curses, short-breathed, gallic,

You spat into their pretty ears before you came;
Gone the ocarinas' plaint from pitch-black foredecks
Under velvet, star-prinked skies, a sound that could unsex
The bosun's mate; the grappling, and the secret shame.

Gone the tall clifftops and the keening of the gulls,
The hungers, fears and lassitudes, the nights you spent
And spent, tossed in sea-fevers that would not relent,
The fire-red latitudes, the stranded, rusting hulls –

The *Zoe, Belle Etoile*; gone the little bar at dawn
That saw you enter love as you once entered water,
Hands outstretched, blind; gone that lovely, dutiful daughter
Who gulped and gulped the star-filled salt flood on Cape Horn,

On the bay of San Francisco and round Sydney Heads…
Forget how she would sketch a column with her mouth
And fingers, then steer your tongue and cock due south
As she had done so often in so many beds;

Forget the fronds of weed that wave like mermaids' hair
In shallow water, and that stark, shadowy blur,
Her pointed, dark isosceles of salt-wet fur,
Forget how white skin joined her suntanned skin just there.

Forget her moods as dull as bruised wet skies, or freaked
With black like pebbles splashed by tar; forget the sun
Going down, the salt that stung you when you moved as one
To the rocking of the waves, the timbers as they creaked.

Forget how winter's light ignited on the sea
And made of it a thousand broken mirrors; how
The whiplashes of salt wind on your burning brow
Would leave you cleansed and giddy, drunk with it, and free.

Forget the sunwarmed tropic, flat calms, deep and shoal,
The ice-packs and the southern seas, fogbound, forlorn,
The long Agulhas combers, greybeards of the Horn,
The bleak and bitter kingdom – the Forties to the Pole.

Forget the Snares, the Westerlies, the Trade that never fails,
And Old Cape Stiff, Trafalgar and the Lizard Light;
The old Pagoda Anchorage, brasses winking bright,
Spars like a forest; and the skippers hard as nails.

Forget the *Falcon, Spindrift*, and the *Fiery Cross,*
Ariel, Leander and proud *Thermopylae,*
Racing home to London River, chests of China tea,
Crack her on for Carrick Roads with dolphin, albatross.

Forget the salted shrunken lakes, the sad deserted shore
You drift towards, and have become; forget how fast
The harbour-lights and dockside bustle turned to past,
A coast no tramp, hold full of water, sets out for.

Forget the stove-in wheelhouse and the splintered compass,
The stone façades that chill you when you're leaving port,
The broken steering gear that snags your every thought,
And how you learned to spit and swear and make a rumpus

As a boy who'd barely left the comfortless lee
Of your mother; forget the fluttered handkerchiefs,
The old hurts and the inextinguishable griefs,
And drop like a pebble through the blue immensity

Of water, your voyage ends in the mermaid's lair
Where all is transfigured, sea-horses and sea-shells
And the sunken piano tuned for your farewells,
And she, the mermaid, is swimming towards you there.

PORT

Lurching over copper-stripped benches,
Hungry Hill and Sugarloaf Mountain moody as Hell,
on Beara Peninsula where walkers pass and massive
trawlers lurk in Castletownberehaven, where soldiers
and fishermen rough it up outside the pubs, language flex,
influx, foothold, the whitefish in the bellies
of ancientness as if it's always there
to call up when things are tough, uncertain,
and hard-but-attractive wives are a captain's luck.

I KNEW THIS PATH, A THIN BROWN ARM AROUND THE CLIFF

I knew this path, a thin brown arm around the cliff,
Small boats pulling off-white wrinkled threads
In the grey silk of sea; a sharp stink like the heads
In our old Thames-side HQ… 'Same old riff:

How you might have made a go of it with her,
Or her; how she threw her thin brown arm
Around you and you felt that unearthly calm,
Au bord de là mer, how much in love you were…

And have you come back? Will you never learn?
That some mistakes are final, that it is too late
To find safe moorings here, or at Chiswick Eyot;
That you should expect the unexpected turn

That leaves you all at sea, the compass shattered –
Remember when you breezed into the Swan,
The Mermaid or the Dove, and how far gone
The ship's complement of women were, how tattered

Everything looked, below decks and above,
How you swayed and swaggered like a buccaneer
Who scented plunder? How you saw all your gear
Go overboard with your learning and your love?'

ST IVES

1.

Tide up across spring neck
pincer of tide and wide wave
riding high over sea defence
to lash concrete and stone
flail and scratch at windows
rub rust into ballast wounds
neap at adjustment as boats
swirl to arrive to escape
sun on clock-face and seaweed
on walkways kinetic wrestling
boat lifted from flanks bleeds
runnels and shuddering pools
keel-hauled over sandy bottom
still as under-water we all see
where so much recirculates
single mast of beheaded ketch
a recollection or maybe
really there as a claim to act
hoping to cut some slack
bob out past lighthouse
and seal pacts

2.

Keels over settles refloats fetch contact stress point
stuck and drowned as muddy hullabaloo below tide
mark diggings castles moats estuaries plastic sharps
the odd half of a bivalve goes and comes round returns
what flow microclimates cases of faith jettisoned
like sea burials where no definite articles take as keeling
over varies by point of withdrawal an imbalance on deck

an outboard motor tilting and favouring one side one
angle of descent how it settles how a flotilla rests
in absence of water as tide diminishes waves hammer
planks and stress bodies of coming in never going out never.

LONG AFTER (*JULIEN GRACQ*)

Round my rusted decks –
Me, the hulk far out
In black howling air –
Her new life breaks
Like a wind-whipped sea,
Her seaweed-and-musk
Envelops me.

I dream at dusk
The shipwrecked sailor's dream,
I search the black waves
The wild skies for a flare
But a sick moon shows
Another's stiff prick ream
Her little clam
Her dark sea-rose
And shows me what I am:

Rusted hulk, two masts
High water covers up,
Two warning blasts
And watery grave.

BRISE MARINE

(after Mallarmé)

The flesh is sad, alas! and I've read all the books.
To fly! Fly south! I sense that birds are drunk
From being amid the unknown spray and skies!
Nothing, not ancient gardens reflected in eyes
Will hold back this heart that steeps itself in ocean
O nights! nor the abandoned gleam of my lantern
On the blank paper guarded by its whiteness,
Nor the young woman with an infant at her breast.
I shall depart! Swaying your masts, steamer,
Weigh anchor for some exotic nature!

This Languor, cruel hopes with no relief,
Still requires the supreme farewell of handkerchiefs!
And, perhaps, the masts, welcoming tempests,
Are of the kind that a wind bends above wrecked ships
Lost, without masts, without masts or fertile isles . . .
But O my heart, listen to the sailors' shanties!

SEA-MUSIC

In one of the forgotten places of the earth,
The end of the Hammersmith and City Line
On a little island made from builders' waste,

Stands a single palm, patched and peeling, tattered
Tropical bird – *its fire-fangled feathers*
Dangle down... As I walk past it to the 8.09

I can hear palms rustle in the tropic airs,
I can hear sea-music, sirens singing,
Snatches of gentle ukulele songs,

The small waves' whisper of *shush, shush;*
I can taste the *tristesse* of a tropical berth,
A warm wind from the barrier-reef bringing

Sticky-sweet of rum, salt of panties and thongs
Those wriggling sirens yanked down in their haste,
The salt-sweetness that is uniquely theirs;

I can see the tattoos – a tiny patch of home,
The shadow-island, parakeet and palm,
Just below the panty-line, above the bush;

Can see the moon through shutters stripe an arm,
Outflung, a flattened breast – the fleck of foam,
The just-fucked look in grey-green eyes, like sea-mist! . . .

A sea wind shakes the palms and rocks the sea-bed
And a faint glow dancing in the fine salt spray
Leads me where I'm led. *This,* the sirens say,

Was not your true course; why did you steer it?
Because to you all places were the same?
Infernal joys, joys of the deadened spirit.

You went to where a tree stood like a flame
That flickered in the petrol-glare; you learnt to fear it.
No place of safety and no berth free from blame.

Infernal joys of night-time, deadened spirit
On your tongue, your tongue hot as a flame
And the insects uttering their prayer. Who would hear it?

You looked for comfort but no comfort came
On the tundra's permafrost. Your deadened spirit
Flickered in the glare of its own shame.

Then they are gone to spindrift, lost in air…
It seems I know this place, each creek and cove
Though when I saw it last, I can't remember:

A wide expanse, flat as the sands at Camber,
Cloud-hung, all paths leading to a concrete pillbox –
Piss-smelling floor, condoms, the ghosts of cocks,

Dried seaweed and turds – not the promised home
Or place of safety! – and a glint like amethyst
In violet eyes – that dutiful daughter…

Could this be where she's decided it must end? –
Not in some hotel bar, black velvet skirt
And pearls, her ash-blond hair cut shorter –

The way I've seen her look up from her glass of wine
And say, 'So you've finally found me, as if I were
A broken toy you'd thrown away and picked up again,

Wondering how much it might cost to mend…
So much pain, so much you're prepared to deny –
What is it, bygones bygones, that old line?

Or are you wondering if I can still be had
For the price of a double at the Grand –
Are you sick or mad? Don't you understand

How much I wanted you, how much it hurt?
How I used to pray you'd come back, or else die
Calling out for me…?' Instead I hear these words,

You will always belong here, no matter where you rove.
Your 'poetry' – still want to be the Baudelaire
De nos jours, *or a cut-price Byron, mad, bad*

And dangerous? Once it would have been the syphilis that got you,
Or opium, or drink – things that would rot you
From the inside out; or a husband would have shot you…

Bid farewell to shipmates who are gone, while you've been spared –
But not for long – and set sail, for those fortunate isles
Where the only commuting is in nautical miles,

Where the men are men and the women are all smiles;
They lie about you, your errors and your wrecks,
One course left open. Set sail. Clear the decks.

BELLE ÉTOILE

(after Paul Louis Rossi)

One more time
I've let myself drift
Through the network of darkened streets
Once more the boat has left harbour
And I've forgotten oars and compass

Mysterious
Women, or statues,
Stone façades or plaster faces
You steal my nights from me
You mix your blood with mine, in spite of me

Nothing welcomes me nothing
In the solitude where I wander
Not a single opening door
And the fluttering of handkerchiefs can't hold me
The current is too strong, the rudder's broken

Let it go give up
Don't stretch out a hand to the drowned man
I'll roll like a pebble to the sea
And don't go grieving over him he has
His eternity of recollection innocence and forgetfulness

In the bitter strictness of the night
The stars are extinguished after so many glances
It's between two waves that the voyage ends
The lighthouses winking to each other on the coast
I'm lit up suddenly like phosphorescence, glowing algae

ACKNOWLEDGEMENTS

Grateful acknowledgements are due to the editors of the following publications, where some of these poems, or earlier versions of them, first appeared:

Archipelago, *Australian Poetry Journal*, the *Canberra Times*, *Drunken Boats* (Sylph Editions / American University of Paris), *Greenheart* (Chatto & Windus, 1990), *Harm* (Chatto & Windus, 1994), *Idaho Review*, *Literary Imagination*, *The London Magazine*, *New England Review*, *New Walk*, *New Welsh Review*, the *Spectator*, the *Times Literary Supplement*, *The Yale Review*.